SOLAR SYSTEM

by Jon Richards

Silver Dolphin

San Diego, California

Silver Dolphin Books
An imprint of the Baker & Taylor Publishing Group
10350 Barnes Canyon Road, San Diego, CA 92121
www.silverdolphinbooks.com

Copyright ©2014 Studio Fun International, Inc.
44 South Broadway, White Plains, NY 10601 U.S.A. and
Studio Fun International Limited,
The Ice House, 124-126 Walcot Street, Bath UK BA1 5BG
All rights reserved.

Text copyright ©2014 Flowerpot Press
Designed by Flowerpot Press
Consultant: Beatrice Mueller, Senior Scientist, Planetary Science Institute

"Silver Dolphin" is a registered trademark of Baker & Taylor.
All rights reserved.

ISBN-13: 978-1-62686-301-9
ISBN-10: 1-62686-301-6

First published in the United States in 2000 by Copper Beech Books, an imprint of
The Millbrook Press, 2 Old New Milford Road, Brookfield, Connecticut 06804

Manufactured, printed, and assembled in China.
1 2 3 4 5 18 17 16 15 14
HH1/07/14

CONTENTS

THE SOLAR SYSTEM

Earth doesn't just hang in space. It zooms at almost 67,000 miles per hour around the Sun. Earth isn't alone. Another seven **planets** circle the Sun, too—all held in place by the pull of the Sun's **gravity**. The Sun, its planets and their **moons**, and **comets** and **asteroids** are together called the solar system.

Scientists established that the solar system formed 4.6 billion years ago. At first, it was just a dark, whirling mass of gas and dust. But as it spun, gravity pulled bits tighter together. The dense center became the Sun, and dust and gas farther out came together to form the planets.

Look for definitions of **bold** words in the glossary.

Neptune

Jupiter

Uranus

DID YOU KNOW?

The solar system is at least 12 billion miles across. If Earth were the size of a grain of salt, the solar system would be as big as a sports stadium.

The four planets closest to the Sun are Mercury, Venus, Earth, and Mars. They are all quite small and are made mainly of rock. The next four are Jupiter, Saturn, Uranus, and Neptune. They are much larger than the four inner planets and are made of hydrogen, helium, and other gases.

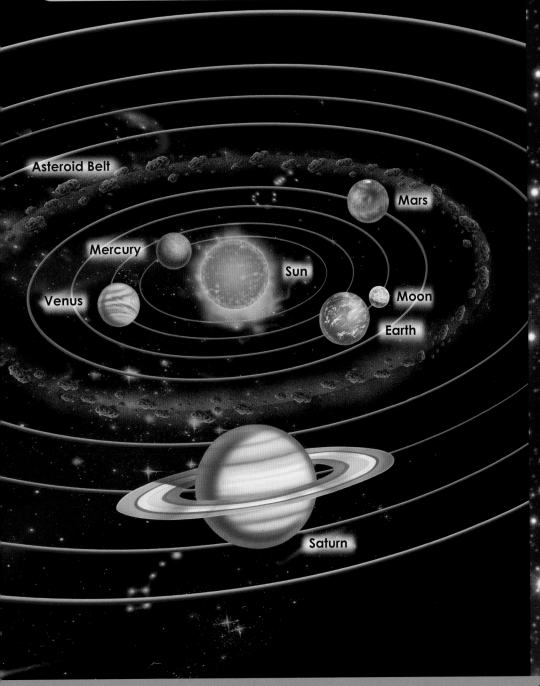

Asteroid Belt

Mars

Mercury

Sun

Venus

Moon

Earth

Saturn

THE SUN

The Sun is a **star**, and like all stars, it is a huge fiery ball. The temperature at the center of the Sun reaches over 28 million°F! That's hot enough to melt any known substance. Energy from the Sun releases heat and light. That energy takes about a million years to rise to the Sun's surface, and then it spreads out quickly into space. The Sun weighs about 333,000 times more than Earth, and is 110 times wider.

Every now and then, huge, looping **plumes** of hot gas erupt from the Sun's surface. These plumes are called solar prominences.

Sunspot

SUN STATS

Average distance from Earth
93 million miles

Diameter
865,000 miles

Temperature at center
28,000,000°F

Temperature at surface
9,900°F

Rotation on axis
25.45 days

Revolution in Milky Way
225 million years

Number of planets
8

DID YOU KNOW?

An area of the Sun's surface the size of a postage stamp shines with the power of 1.5 million candles! This is why the Sun is bright enough to light up Earth, 93 million miles away.

MERCURY

Mercury is the nearest planet to the Sun, on average about 36 million miles away. Mercury has little **atmosphere**, so the side facing the Sun can reach more than 800°F, while the dark side is an icy-cold -300°F.

Mercury is small, so its gravity is very weak and can't hold onto an atmosphere. There is nothing to protect the planet from the Sun's rays or to stop **meteoroids** from bashing into it. As a result, it is deeply dented with **craters**. A journey across the surface would show you nothing more than vast, empty valleys; cliffs hundreds of miles long; and yellow dust everywhere.

Every so often, Mercury passes across the face of the Sun, when seen from Earth.

Earth turns once around on its **axis** in 23 hours and 56 minutes. Mercury takes nearly 59 Earth days to turn once around its axis.

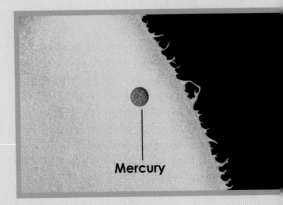

Mercury

Mercury **rotates** slowly, but revolves around the Sun in just 88 days (compared to 365 days for Earth). As it turns slowly away from the Sun, it whizzes around the other side, so that the sunny side is still facing the Sun.

Like Earth, Mercury has polar ice caps of frozen water under a layer of dark material.

Earth

Mercury

Mercury is smaller than some of Jupiter's moons. It is 20 times lighter than and about 40 percent the size of Earth.

MERCURY STATS

Average distance from Sun
36 million miles

Diameter
3,029 miles

Surface temperature
−300°F to 800°F

Rotation on axis
58.6 hours

Revolution around Sun
88 days

Number of moons
0

Tilt of axis
0°

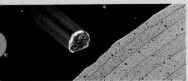

The Caloris Basin is a large crater on Mercury's surface. It was formed when a 100-mile-wide rock collided with the planet.

The crash made a crater 800 miles wide. Rings of mountains were pushed up around the crater's edge by the force of this crash.

The crash also caused lava from Mercury's mantle to spill out onto the crater floor, flattening its surface.

DID YOU KNOW?

Mercury's craters are named after famous writers, artists, and composers.

VENUS

Venus is almost the same size as Earth. It measures about 7,500 miles across and weighs just a little less than Earth. It is sometimes called the "Evening Star" or the "Morning Star." This is because it is quite close to the Sun, and can be seen in the night sky just after sunset or just before sunrise.

The surface of Venus can't be seen, since it is hidden under a thick layer of clouds. It has probably always been too hot for water to have existed there. All that is left are hot, bone-dry, rolling plains dotted with volcanoes and vast **plateaus**.

Venus is a beautiful planet, covered in swirls of pinkish-white clouds. The pink clouds are actually made partly of sulfuric acid. They are so thick that they press down on the planet's surface hard enough to crush a car!

Carbon dioxide in Venus's atmosphere traps heat on the surface, boosting the temperature to as high as 867°F, the hottest planet surface temperature in the solar system.

Venus

Moon

When our Moon is a new **crescent** moon, it is between Earth and the Sun. Venus lies between Earth and the Sun, too. So sometimes you will see Venus near the new Moon as it rises.

Venus is one of only two planets (with Uranus) that rotates in a clockwise direction. This is called retrograde rotation.

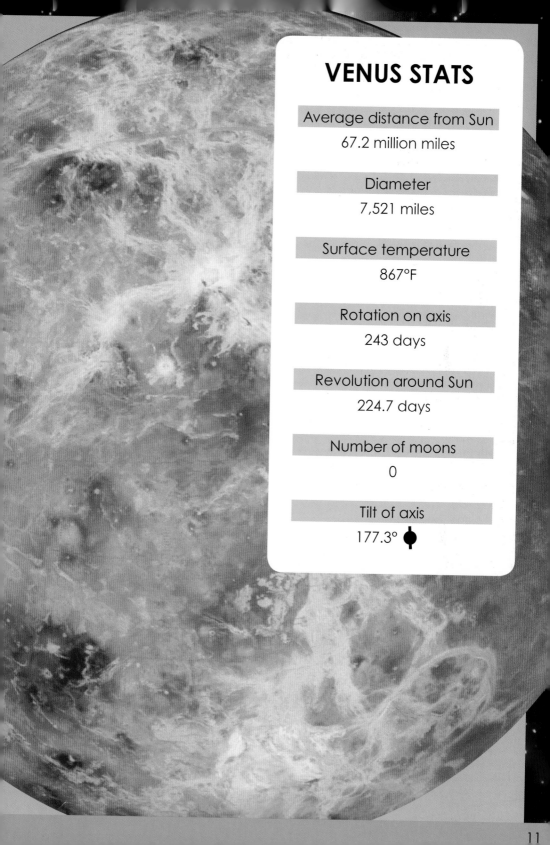

VENUS STATS

Average distance from Sun	
67.2 million miles	
Diameter	
7,521 miles	
Surface temperature	
867°F	
Rotation on axis	
243 days	
Revolution around Sun	
224.7 days	
Number of moons	
0	
Tilt of axis	
177.3°	

EARTH

Earth is the third planet out from the Sun, about 93 million miles away. It is not so close to the Sun that it is scorching hot, nor so far away that it is icy cold. It has water on its surface, and can sustain life.

Earth is a special place. About 70 percent of its surface is covered by water, and water makes life possible. It also has a layer of gases, called the atmosphere, in which we breathe.

Earth is made mainly of rock and is the **densest** planet in the solar system. But it is not just a solid ball. It has a shell, or crust, of hard rock. Beneath that is a layer about 1,850 miles deep of warm, partly melted rock called the mantle. The center is a **core** made entirely of hot metal—mostly iron.

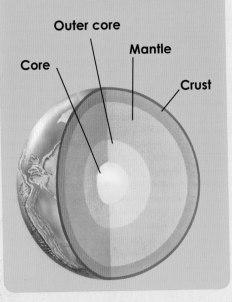

Outer core

Mantle

Core

Crust

Most of the surface of Earth is ocean. Can you spot the land?

EARTH STATS

Average distance from Sun
93 million miles

Diameter
7,926 miles

Surface temperature
-128.6°F to 136°F

Rotation on axis
23 hours, 56 minutes (1day)

Revolution around Sun
365.25 days

Number of moons
1

Tilt of axis
23.45°

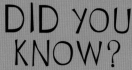 DID YOU KNOW?

Earth is not quite round. It bulges at the middle, around the **equator**. Passing through Earth from **pole** to pole is 27 miles shorter than going between opposite points on the equator.

THE MOON

The Moon is Earth's closest companion. It is about 240,000 miles away. The Moon circles around Earth about once a month. It is a barren, lifeless place covered with dust and craters caused by large meteoroids crashing into it billions of years ago.

The Moon appears to change shape over the course of a month. We only see the side of the Moon that is lit by the Sun. As the Moon circles Earth, we see it from different angles—and so see more or less of its sunlit side.

At the beginning of the cycle (1), we see a thin, crescent-shaped sliver. This grows over the next two weeks to a full moon (3), when we see all the sunlit side. It then shrinks back over the rest of the cycle to a crescent shape—the old moon (5).

1
2
3
4
5

Amazingly, the Moon was probably made by a space collision. About 4.5 billion years ago, soon after Earth formed, a planet at least as big as Mars collided with Earth. The crash completely melted the other planet, and splashes flew off into space. Gradually, gravity pulled these splashes together into a ball, which cooled to form the Moon.

A large object hits Earth. The object melts, and splashes of **debris** fly into space.

The debris spins in **orbit** and joins together to form the Moon.

DID YOU KNOW? ?

The first person to set foot on the Moon was astronaut Neil Armstrong in July 1969.

The Moon's surface

MARS

Mars is a barren planet, with no oceans—just red rocks and dust and a pink sky. The daytime temperatures on Mars are similar to the temperatures on Earth.

In the 1880s, astronomers thought dark lines they saw on the surface of Mars were actually canals built by Martians. They proved to be optical illusions, but the existence of valleys shows that water once flowed over the surface in abundance.

MARS STATS

Average distance from Sun
142 million miles

Diameter
4,220 miles

Surface temperature
-220°F to 80°F

Rotation on axis
24.6 hours

Revolution around Sun
687 Earth days

Number of moons
2

Tilt of axis
25.2°

Ice-covered pole

More spacecraft have landed on Mars than on any other planet. In 1997 the Mars Pathfinder landed and sent out a robotic truck to scan the area and beam back images. In 2012 the Curiosity rover landed on Mars for a two-year search for signs of life.

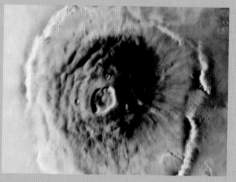

Like Earth and Venus, Mars has volcanoes. In fact, Olympus Mons on Mars is the biggest volcano in the solar system—it is three times higher than Earth's highest mountain, Mount Everest.

THE ASTEROID BELT

The asteroid belt is a band of rocky and metallic objects that stretches between Mars and Jupiter. It is about 100 million miles wide! The objects are called asteroids. Some of them are over 100 miles across, and others are only a few inches wide. There are millions of asteroids in the asteroid belt. These asteroids orbit around the Sun, just like the planets.

Asteroid belt

Jupiter

Sun

— Mars

Computer model of the asteroid belt
as seen from above

When asteroids get too close to Earth, they usually burn up in
Earth's atmosphere. Sometimes a fragment does reach the
ground, leaving a large crater like this one near Winslow,
Arizona. It is 600 feet deep and nearly a mile across.

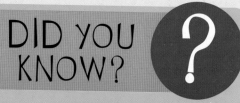

DID YOU
KNOW? **?**

More than 20,000 asteroids in the belt
have been named.

JUPITER

Jupiter is gigantic. It is by far the biggest planet in the solar system—over 88,000 miles across—and it takes 12 years to go around the Sun. It is an enormous ball of gas, more like the Sun than like Earth, and is made mainly of hydrogen and helium. You can see it clearly for part of the year—it is brighter than any of the stars. At the center of Jupiter is a dense core, up to 40 times the mass of Earth.

In addition to having many moons, Jupiter, like Saturn, has a number of rings. However, the rings around Jupiter are nothing like those around Saturn.

Jupiter's Largest Moons

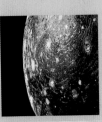

Europa	Io	Ganymede	Callisto

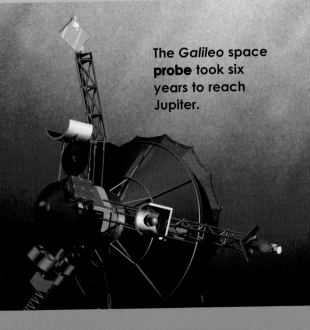

The *Galileo* space probe took six years to reach Jupiter.

The Great Red Spot

JUPITER STATS

Average distance from Sun
483 million miles

Diameter
88,855 miles

Surface temperature
-227°F

Rotation on axis
9.9 hours

Revolution around Sun
11.86 years

Number of moons
67

Tilt of axis
3.12°

DID YOU KNOW?

The Great Red Spot that you can see on Jupiter is actually a hurricane-like storm that is nearly 25,000 miles wide!

JUPITER'S MOONS

Jupiter has 67 confirmed moons. The four largest (Io, Europa, Ganymede, and Callisto) were discovered by the scientist Galileo in 1610. Ganymede and Callisto are larger than our own Moon, and the other two are not much smaller.

Until Galileo saw through his telescope that Jupiter's moons circled around it, people thought that everything in the universe revolved around our Earth.

Ganymede

If you were on Ganymede, you would see Jupiter in the sky.

Europa has a very bright, smooth surface of ice, possibly with liquid water beneath. Scientists think that there might be life-forms in this water. In places, the surface of Europa is cracked like an eggshell.

Callisto

Io

DID YOU KNOW?

Callisto's Valhalla crater is so dark, it makes the moon look like a giant eyeball!

Io has been called the most volcanic body in the solar system. When the *Voyager 2* space probe passed it in 1979, it discovered that plumes of material were being shot out from Io's surface up to a height of nearly 200 miles. It was the first evidence of active volcanoes anywhere other than Earth.

SATURN

Saturn is the second-largest planet, a gas giant over 74,000 miles across. Saturn is known as the "Ringed Planet" because around it circle amazing rings. Saturn's core is made of rock twice as hot as the Sun's surface.

When Galileo first discovered Saturn's rings in 1610, he thought the planet had "ears" or "handles" because his telescope wasn't sharp enough.

SATURN STATS

Average distance from Sun
890,000,000 miles

Diameter
74,896 miles

Surface temperature
-285°F

Rotation on axis
10.6 hours

Revolution around Sun
29.4 years

Number of moons
62

Tilt of axis
26.7°

Saturn's rings are bands of billions of tiny blocks of ice and dust, circling the planet endlessly. Each ring is thousands of miles wide (except for one called the "F Ring," which is only 500 miles wide).

Changing Rings

1995

2000

2005

2010

2015

We see Saturn at different angles at different times, so we can see Saturn's rings better at some times than others. In 2010 the rings were edge-on and hard to see. In 2015 they will be at a greater angle, giving us a clear view.

DID YOU KNOW?

Saturn is so light that it would float in a giant bathtub of water!

SATURN'S MOONS

Iapetus

Like Jupiter, Saturn has a large number of moons. At least 62 have been identified, and there are probably more smaller ones still to be discovered. Titan (shown off in the distance) is the largest of all Saturn's moons, and is the second-largest moon in the solar system after Jupiter's moon Ganymede.

Phoebe

Saturn's moon Mimas shows clearly a huge crater called the Herschel crater. The impact that made the crater was so strong that it almost broke Mimas apart.

One of Saturn's moons, Iapetus, has one side that is dark black like tar, while the other side is white as snow.

DID YOU KNOW? ?

Titan is the only moon with a dense atmosphere, and it is orange!

Dione

Most of Saturn's moons circle quite closely. They all orbit outside Saturn's rings. Phoebe orbits the farthest out, much farther than the other moons, taking 550 days to go around once. It also orbits backward, in an opposite direction to the other moons.

Titan

Saturn

Mimas

Tethys

Herschel crater on Mimas

URANUS

Uranus is so far from the Sun that its atmospheric temperatures drop to -355°F. In this amazing cold, the methane (natural gas) that covers the planet turns to liquid oceans, thousands of miles deep. It is the methane gas that gives this planet its beautiful blue color.

Uranus is almost 2 billion miles from the Sun. This far out, the distance Uranus has to travel around the Sun is vast—and takes about 84 Earth years.

This planet tilts so far that it's on its side. It spins around once every 17 hours, but this has no effect on the length of a day. Instead, the day depends on where Uranus is in its orbit. When the south pole is pointing directly at the Sun, the Sun doesn't go down there for 20 years!

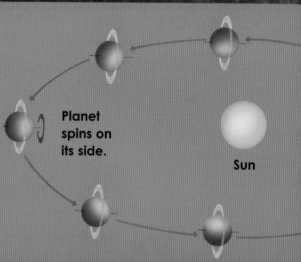

Planet spins on its side.

Sun

DID YOU KNOW?

Uranus is the coldest planet. It is closer to the Sun than Neptune, but its core doesn't radiate much heat.

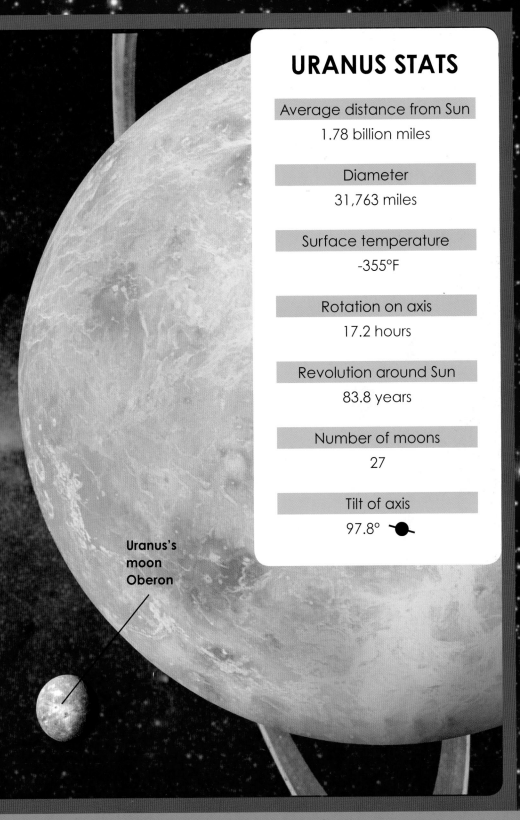

URANUS STATS

Average distance from Sun
1.78 billion miles

Diameter
31,763 miles

Surface temperature
-355°F

Rotation on axis
17.2 hours

Revolution around Sun
83.8 years

Number of moons
27

Tilt of axis
97.8°

Uranus's moon Oberon

NEPTUNE

Neptune is the fourth-largest planet in the solar system. It's so far from the Sun—about 2.8 billion miles—that it takes 163.9 years to go around the Sun.

Neptune has raging storms and clouds on its surface that come and go over the years, probably driven by Neptune's internal heat. It also has a small white cloud of methane ice crystals that zips around the planet once every 16 hours.

Neptune is an icy blue planet with an atmosphere like Uranus, and might have a liquid layer. On Neptune, surface temperatures plunge to -355°F—but its moon Triton is even colder, with temperatures a chilling -393°F. Triton's surface is covered in volcanoes that erupt ice!

DID YOU KNOW?

Neptune is the windiest place in the solar system, with wind speeds of over 1,500 miles per hour—faster than the fastest jet plane.

The Great Dark Spot can sometimes be seen on Neptune's surface.

Triton

NEPTUNE STATS

Average distance from Sun
2.8 billion miles

Diameter
30,775 miles

Surface temperature
-355°F

Rotation on axis
16.1 hours

Revolution around Sun
163.9 years

Number of moons
13

Tilt of axis
28.3°

Artist's rendition of the surface of Triton

DWARF PLANETS

Did you know that our solar system used to have nine planets? Now there are only eight! So what happened? In 1930 scientists discovered an object over 4 billion miles away. They called it a planet because it was big and orbited the Sun, and named it Pluto. But in 2005, astronomers discovered Eris, another object in space that orbits the Sun, and is even farther away than Pluto! Astronomers decided to create a new category instead of adding a tenth planet to our solar system. Pluto and Eris were named dwarf planets.

Pluto

Scientists have found and named five dwarf planets: Pluto, Eris, Ceres, Haumea, and Makemake. But there are over 100 objects in our solar system that astronomers may be able to call dwarf planets—they have a lot of work ahead of them to figure it out!

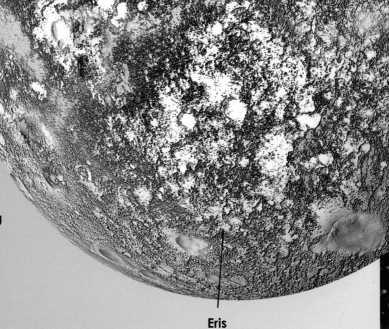

ke planets,
varf planets
bit the Sun and
ve enough
avity to make
em round in shape.
hat makes them
fferent than planets is
at they have other
objects orbiting along
with them.

Eris

DID YOU KNOW? ?

Many planetary scientists still believe that Pluto should be classified as a planet.

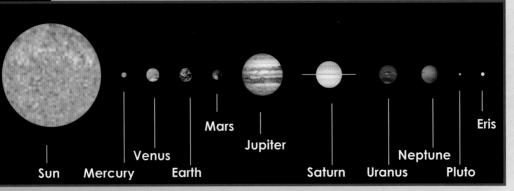

Sun   Mercury   Venus   Earth   Mars   Jupiter   Saturn   Uranus   Neptune   Pluto   Eris

Position of planets and dwarf planets

Comets are like huge, dirty snowballs that orbit in the outer reaches of the solar system. The solid part of a comet, called the **nucleus**, is often only a few miles across, but when it swings in close to the Sun its ices go from solid to gas, causing it to throw out a vast tail of dust and gas.

The center of a comet is a hard core made of ice, frozen gases, and pieces of rock and dust. Around the core are layers of ice and rock. Sometimes it is surrounded by patches of an outer crust.

Halley's Comet appears in the Bayeux Tapestry, which depicts the Battle of Hastings in 1066, but records show that the comet was spotted as long ago as 240 BC.

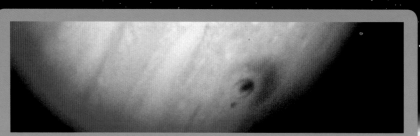

In July 1994, people on Earth watched as fragments of the comet Shoemaker-Levy 9 collided with Jupiter. The comet's impact left a large spot which can clearly be seen on the planet's surface.

Halley's Comet appears in our sky every 76 years or so. In 1986 the space probe *Giotto* was sent up to visit Halley's Comet when it flew past Earth. It flew through the comet, taking photographs as it went.

DID YOU KNOW? ?

In the past, comets were considered bad omens.

METEOROIDS AND SHOOTING STARS

A meteoroid is a very small asteroid. It can be seen as a **meteor**, or shooting star, as it burns in Earth's atmosphere. Most burn away before they fall to Earth. When meteors fall to Earth, they are called meteorites, and are usually no bigger than a lump of coal.

A meteorite is space debris that has fallen to Earth, sometimes leaving a large hole or crater. Most meteorites are quite small and are made of stone or iron. Museums keep collections of meteorites that you can go and see.

It is thought that the impact of a huge asteroid or comet 65 million years ago may have changed conditions on Earth so much that it caused a mass extinction.

The Meteor Crater in Arizona is a vast bowl that formed when a meteorite crashed there 50,000 years ago. The impact created a hole nearly 4,000 feet across and 650 feet deep.

If you look into the night sky at any time of the year, you may see some shooting stars. However, the best time to see good showers of them in the Northern **Hemisphere** is in the first part of August.

DID YOU KNOW?

A very bright shooting star is called a fireball.

SPACE TRAVEL

A human traveled into space for the first time in 1961 when the Soviet Union sent an astronaut, Yuri Gagarin, into orbit around the Earth for almost two hours.

One of the most famous space explorations is the first Moon landing. In July 1969, the United States sent Neil Armstrong, Michael Collins, and Buzz Aldrin into space aboard the *Apollo 11*. Neil Armstrong became the first person to step on the Moon, and said the famous phrase, "That's one small step for man, one giant leap for mankind."

Since 2000, astronauts have been able to work in space aboard the International Space Station, a huge satellite orbiting Earth. Maybe their discoveries will help you travel to space one day!

Today, astronauts from all over the world live and work in the International Space Station.

DID YOU KNOW? ❓

In 1949 a monkey named Albert II went into space!

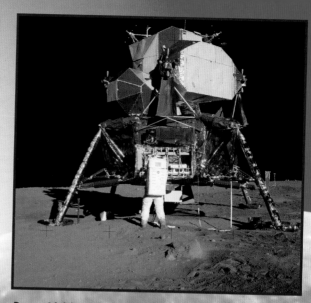

Buzz Aldrin and the Lunar Module

Buzz Aldrin salutes the U.S. flag.

THE MILKY WAY

Our Sun is just one of about 400 billion stars grouped together in a **galaxy** called the Milky Way.
The Milky Way is one of more than 30 billion spiral galaxies in the **universe**.

Canis Major

Puppis

Vela

Carina

Centaurus

Crux

Muca

Triangulum
Australe

Ara

DID YOU KNOW? ?

Scientists think there is a huge black hole in the middle of the Milky Way.

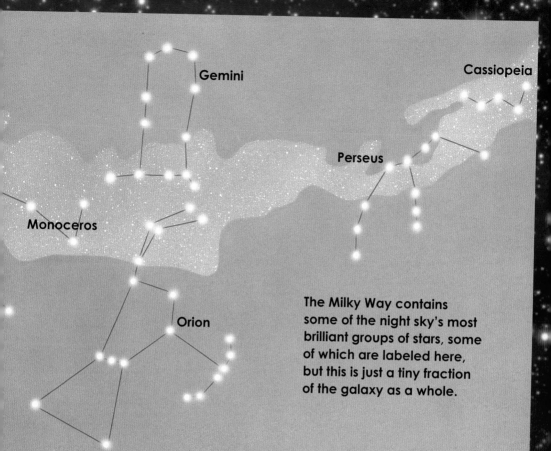

Gemini

Cassiopeia

Perseus

Monoceros

Orion

The Milky Way contains some of the night sky's most brilliant groups of stars, some of which are labeled here, but this is just a tiny fraction of the galaxy as a whole.

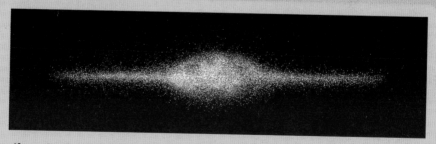

If you're far from town on a dark, clear night, you can see a hazy band of light stretching across the sky. You are actually seeing an edge-on view of the Milky Way galaxy with its countless stars. People long ago called it the Milky Way because it looked like someone had spilled milk across the sky.

SUPERSTRUCTURES

Just as **clusters** of stars form galaxies, galaxies group to form even larger structures. Our Milky Way galaxy is over 100,000 light-years across, but it is just part of a group of 40 galaxies called the Local Group.

Just as galaxies form the Local Group, the Local Group is clumped with other groups of galaxies to form clusters of thousands of galaxies. Half a dozen or so clusters are, in turn, grouped into large superclusters 200 million light-years across.

Local Group

Milky Way

Cluster of
galaxies

Superclusters

Superclusters are grouped in loops
and superwalls, separated by voids
400 million light-years across.

DID YOU KNOW?

The biggest known structure in the
universe is the Great Wall. It is a
superwall, a group of superclusters,
some 500 million light-years long, but
even this may not be the biggest
structure; there may even be
structures 3 billion light-years across!

CONSTELLATIONS

In ancient times, people noticed star patterns in the sky that looked like pictures. People have always made up stories about the stars, linking them into groups and naming them after characters. These groups are called **constellations**. Astronomers recognize 88 in all.

Orion, one of the most famous constellations, is named after the great hunter from Greek legend. Another constellation, Hercules, shares its name with a hero from Roman myth.

You've probably looked up at night and seen the Big Dipper. It is one of the most well-known constellations in the Northern Hemisphere. But did you know it is also called Ursa Major? The name means "large bear." The stars form a bear with a long tail that looks like the handle of a ladle, and that's how it got its nickname, the Big Dipper.

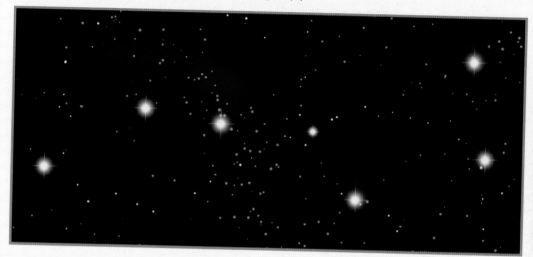

Ursa Major

If you haven't seen the Big Dipper, it might be because it is not visible where you are. Different constellations can be seen in the Northern and Southern Hemispheres, and some constellations are visible in both, but since the Earth is always moving, you will notice different constellations at different times of the year.

Ursa Minor, Orion, and Crux Australis

STAR CHARTS

These charts show the constellations that you can see in the night sky at different times of the year. The map below shows the Northern Hemisphere sky, and the map on the right shows the Southern Hemisphere sky.

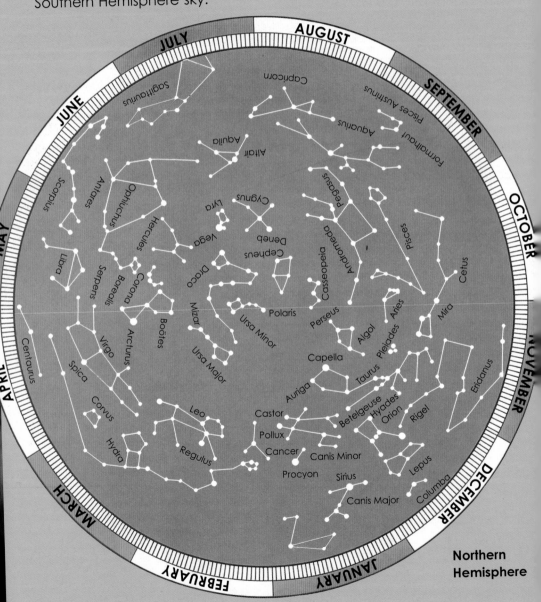

Northern Hemisphere

Southern
Hemisphere

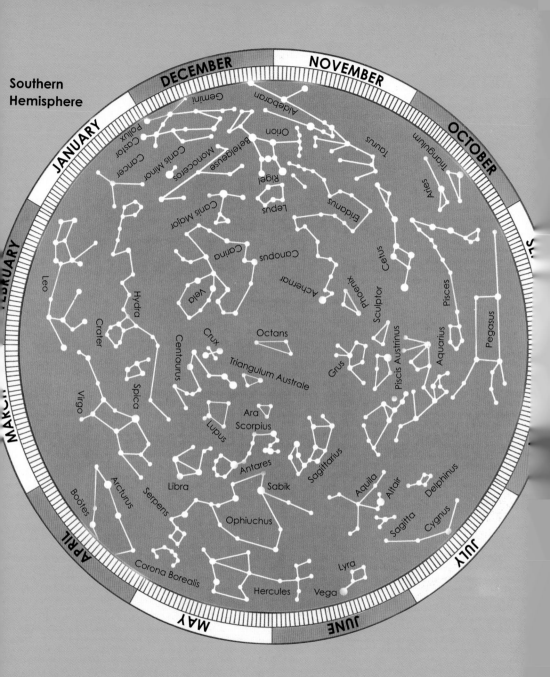

To use the chart, hold it in front of you and make sure the current month is at the bottom. If you are in the Southern Hemisphere, face north. If you are in the Northern Hemisphere, face south.

THE UNIVERSE

The universe is very big—bigger than anything you can possibly imagine. It is not just all the stars, planets, and galaxies, but all the empty space in between. In fact, the universe is everything that exists, from the tiniest bit of an atom to entire galaxies.

No one knows just how big the universe is, or even whether it has a definite edge. Some astronomers think it goes on forever. Others believe it is shaped like a doughnut. But with powerful telescopes, scientists can see incredibly bright objects called **quasars**, which they believe may be on the edge of the universe. These could be as far as 7.45 billion trillion miles away.

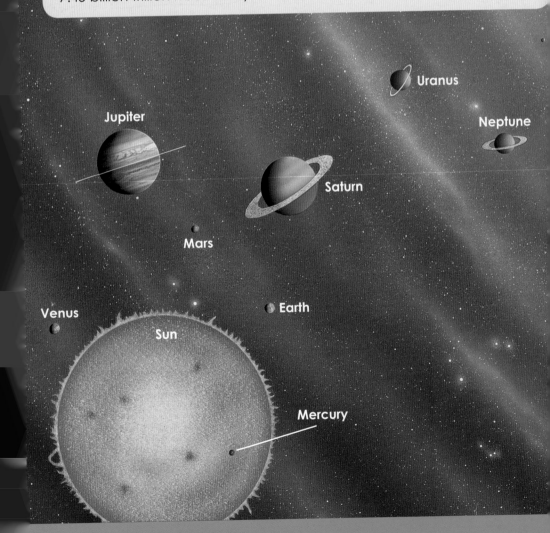

Uranus

Jupiter

Neptune

Saturn

Mars

Venus

Earth

Sun

Mercury

Our galaxy, the Milky Way, seems huge, but the universe contains at least 100 billion galaxies like ours.

DID YOU KNOW?

The universe is mostly empty space.

THE BIG BANG

Scientists suggest that the universe began with an enormous explosion. One moment there was nothing, the next, there was a tiny, unbelievably hot, dense ball, containing all the **matter** in the universe today. Then a moment later, the universe existed, blasting itself into life with the biggest explosion of all time—the big bang.

Every galaxy in the universe is zooming away from ours. This shows that the universe is expanding. By plotting back to the past how rapidly it has been expanding, astronomers have calculated that the universe began about 13 billion years ago.

1. No one knows quite how it started, but scientists think it all began with a small, incredibly hot ball. In the first split second, this grew to the size of a football, and then cooled down rapidly.

2. Gravity behaved very strangely. Instead of pulling things together, it blew them apart, and the universe expanded rapidly. In a split second, it grew bigger than a galaxy.

3. As the universe expanded, it cooled, and tiny particles of energy and matter began to appear. These particles formed a dense, immensely thick soup.

4. After about three minutes, gravity began to behave as it does now, drawing things together. Particles joined to make atoms, and atoms joined to make gases, such as hydrogen and helium.

5. Gases clumped into clouds. After several hundred million years, these clouds began to form stars and galaxies. These galaxies merged into clusters and superclusters, and much later the Sun and solar system were formed. The universe is still expanding, and new planets and stars are still being formed.

GLOSSARY

Asteroid: Small, rocky objects that orbit the Sun in a band between Mars and Jupiter.

Atmosphere: The layer of gases that surrounds a planet. The atmosphere around Earth supplies us with the oxygen that keeps us alive.

Axis: An imaginary line through the center of a planet, moon, or star. The planet, moon, or star spins, or rotates, on this axis.

Cluster: A close group of stars or galaxies.

Comet: An object made of ice and dust that orbits the Sun.

Constellation: A group of stars in the night sky that is named after an animal, object, or mythical figure.

Core: The central part of an object. The Earth's core is made of metal.

Crater: A bowl-shaped hole on the surface of a planet. Some are caused by volcanoes, and some by the impact of a meteorite, asteroid, or comet.

Crescent: Something that has a curved shape.

Debris: The remains of anything after it has been broken down or destroyed.

Dense: Closely packed together.

Equator: An imaginary line that runs around the middle of a planet at an equal distance from its two poles.

Galaxy: A very large group of stars. Our solar system is in the Milky Way galaxy.

Gravity: The force that attracts one object to another. Gravity holds planets and moons in orbit. It also keeps us on the ground.

Hemisphere: Earth is divided by the equator into the Northern and Southern Hemispheres.

Matter: Any material that exists and takes up space.

Meteoroid: A small asteroid that orbits in space.

Meteor: A small, solid body that moves with great speed from space into the Earth's atmosphere, where it burns up.

Moon: Any small body that revolves around a planet.

Nucleus: The central core of an object.

Orbit: The path of an object, such as a planet or a comet, around another object such as a star.

Planet: A large body that orbits the Sun.

Plateau: An area of high, flat ground.

Plume: Something that spreads out in a shape that looks like a feather.

Pole: A point on a planet's surface around which the planet spins or rotates.

Probe: A robotic spacecraft sent from Earth to explore an object in space.

Quasar: An object in space that releases an enormous amount of energy. Quasars are thought to be the centers of very distant galaxies.

Rotate: To turn on, or around, a central point, or axis.

Star: A large ball of gas in the universe that produces light and heat.

Universe: Everything that exists, from the tiniest atoms to entire galaxies and beyond.

Model Assembly Instructions

Sun   Mercury   Venus   Earth   Mars

All of the planets are assembled in the same way.

1. Punch out the four pieces that make one planet.

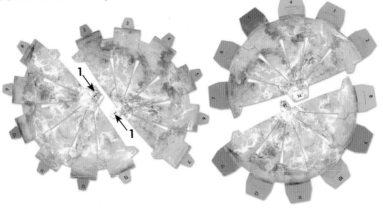

2. Start with the two pieces that have tabs labeled 1.

3. Attach the pieces together by sliding tab 1 into slot 1.

4. Now begin to join the pie shaped sections together by joining each set of tabs.

5. You will see that the pieces will begin to curve and form a half sphere.

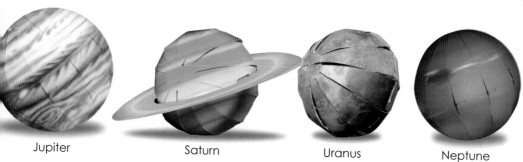

Jupiter   Saturn   Uranus   Neptune

6. Repeat the same process with the two pieces that have tabs labeled 14. You now have two half spheres.

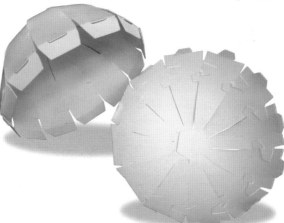

7. Join the two half spheres together by matching the corresponding tabs and slots (2 to 13).

   Your planet is finished!

Saturn

1. Saturn has one extra step and piece.

2. Punch out the ring and insert your finished planet inside the ring.

3. Insert the tabs into the slots to hold the ring in place.

   Your Saturn is finished!

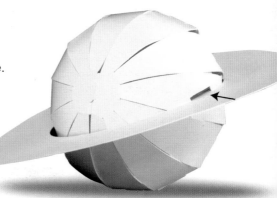

Photo Credits

Illustrations by Jeremy Pyke, Nick Hawken, Ian Thompson, Mike Saunders, Peter Kesteven, Graham White, Simon Tegg, Colin Howard, Alex Pang and Richard Rockwood.
Photos from *The Awesome Book of the Universe* and National Aeronautics and Space Administration (NASA) except where indicated: border, p. 1 and throughout: Shutterstock/ peresanz; border, p. 4 and throughout: Shutterstock/AstroStar; p. 34-35, Shutterstock/ Paul Fleet; p. 36-37, Shutterstock/pixbox77